SOLA GRATIA CO.
FOR THE THEOLOGIAN IN HER

I have hidden your word in my heart,
that I might not sin against you.

Psalm 119:11

This journal belongs to:

_____

Read. Write. Love.
TRUTH

SPEAKER _____

DATE ____ / ____ / ____

KEY SCRIPTURES: _____ _____ _____

main points

WRITE OUT VERSE-BY-VERSE

KEYWORDS/DEFINITIONS

verse-by-verse

WRITE OUT VERSE-BY-VERSE

KEYWORDS / DEFINITIONS

verse-by-verse

THEOLOGICAL / DOCTRINAL TRUTHS I FOUND

WHAT DID I LEARN ABOUT GOD'S CHARACTER?

HOW WILL I LIVE IN LIGHT OF THIS TRUTH?

My Prayer Journal

MY FAMILY

Violet to know and love Jesus

Behavior is bigger than feelings

Colton peace and car resolution

MY CHURCH

Volunteers

Unity - community

MY FRIENDS

Karen & Caroline truth

Susan Chesson

Emily's birthday & quarantine

MY COMMUNITY

Amber & Sebastian - loss of family members

Jenna D. interview

MY NATION

COVID

THE WORLD

COVID

pray continually

Greyson & Noah continued development

Abigail and Job, apartment

Caleb & throat pain

Sam & Jonathan

answered prayers

Read. Write. Love.
TRUTH

SPEAKER _____

DATE ___ / ___ / ___

KEY SCRIPTURES: _____ _____ _____

main points

WRITE OUT VERSE-BY-VERSE

KEYWORDS / DEFINITIONS

verse-by-verse

WRITE OUT VERSE-BY-VERSE   KEYWORDS/DEFINITIONS

verse-by-verse

THEOLOGICAL/DOCTRINAL TRUTHS I FOUND

WHAT DID I LEARN ABOUT GOD'S CHARACTER?

HOW WILL I LIVE IN LIGHT OF THIS TRUTH?

My Prayer Journal

MY FAMILY	MY CHURCH	MY FRIENDS

MY COMMUNITY	MY NATION	THE WORLD

pray continually	answered prayers

Read. Write. Love.
TRUTH

KEY SCRIPTURES: _____ _____ _____

main points

WRITE OUT VERSE-BY-VERSE

KEYWORDS / DEFINITIONS

verse-by-verse

WRITE OUT VERSE-BY-VERSE

KEYWORDS / DEFINITIONS

verse-by-verse

THEOLOGICAL / DOCTRINAL TRUTHS I FOUND

WHAT DID I LEARN ABOUT GOD'S CHARACTER?

HOW WILL I LIVE IN LIGHT OF THIS TRUTH?

My Prayer Journal

MY FAMILY	MY CHURCH	MY FRIENDS

MY COMMUNITY	MY NATION	THE WORLD

pray continually

answered prayers

Read. Write. Love.
TRUTH

SPEAKER _____

DATE _____ / _____ / _____

KEY SCRIPTURES: _____ _____ _____

main points

WRITE OUT VERSE-BY-VERSE

KEYWORDS / DEFINITIONS

verse-by-verse

WRITE OUT VERSE-BY-VERSE

KEYWORDS / DEFINITIONS

verse-by-verse

THEOLOGICAL / DOCTRINAL TRUTHS I FOUND

WHAT DID I LEARN ABOUT GOD'S CHARACTER?

HOW WILL I LIVE IN LIGHT OF THIS TRUTH?

My Prayer Journal

_____ / _____ / _____

DATE

MY FAMILY

MY CHURCH

MY FRIENDS

MY COMMUNITY

MY NATION

THE WORLD

pray continually

answered prayers

Read. Write. Love.
TRUTH

SPEAKER _____   DATE ___ / ___ / ___

KEY SCRIPTURES: _____ _____ _____

main points

WRITE OUT VERSE-BY-VERSE

KEYWORDS / DEFINITIONS

verse-by-verse

WRITE OUT VERSE-BY-VERSE

KEYWORDS/DEFINITIONS

verse-by-verse

THEOLOGICAL/DOCTRINAL TRUTHS I FOUND

WHAT DID I LEARN ABOUT GOD'S CHARACTER?

HOW WILL I LIVE IN LIGHT OF THIS TRUTH?

My Prayer Journal

MY FAMILY	MY CHURCH	MY FRIENDS

MY COMMUNITY	MY NATION	THE WORLD

pray continually

answered prayers

Read. Write. Love.
TRUTH

SPEAKER _____

DATE _____ / _____ / _____

KEY SCRIPTURES: _____ _____ _____

main points

WRITE OUT VERSE-BY-VERSE

KEYWORDS / DEFINITIONS

verse-by-verse

WRITE OUT VERSE-BY-VERSE   KEYWORDS/DEFINITIONS

verse-by-verse

THEOLOGICAL/DOCTRINAL TRUTHS I FOUND

WHAT DID I LEARN ABOUT GOD'S CHARACTER?

HOW WILL I LIVE IN LIGHT OF THIS TRUTH?

My Prayer Journal

DATE _____ / ___ / ___

MY FAMILY	MY CHURCH	MY FRIENDS

MY COMMUNITY	MY NATION	THE WORLD

pray continually

answered prayers

Read. Write. Love.
TRUTH

KEY SCRIPTURES: _____   _____   _____

main points

WRITE OUT VERSE-BY-VERSE

KEYWORDS / DEFINITIONS

verse-by-verse

WRITE OUT VERSE-BY-VERSE

KEYWORDS / DEFINITIONS

verse-by-verse

THEOLOGICAL / DOCTRINAL TRUTHS I FOUND

WHAT DID I LEARN ABOUT GOD'S CHARACTER?

HOW WILL I LIVE IN LIGHT OF THIS TRUTH?

My Prayer Journal

DATE ____ / ____ / ____

MY FAMILY

MY CHURCH

MY FRIENDS

MY COMMUNITY

MY NATION

THE WORLD

pray continually

answered prayers

Read. Write. Love.
TRUTH

SPEAKER _____ DATE ____ / ____ / ____

KEY SCRIPTURES: _____ _____ _____

main points

WRITE OUT VERSE-BY-VERSE

KEYWORDS / DEFINITIONS

verse-by-verse

WRITE OUT VERSE-BY-VERSE   KEYWORDS / DEFINITIONS

verse-by-verse

THEOLOGICAL / DOCTRINAL TRUTHS I FOUND

WHAT DID I LEARN ABOUT GOD'S CHARACTER?

HOW WILL I LIVE IN LIGHT OF THIS TRUTH?

My Prayer Journal

_____ / _____ / _____
DATE

| MY FAMILY | MY CHURCH | MY FRIENDS |

| MY COMMUNITY | MY NATION | THE WORLD |

pray continually

answered prayers

Read. Write. Love.
TRUTH

KEY SCRIPTURES: _____ _____ _____

main points

WRITE OUT VERSE-BY-VERSE

KEYWORDS / DEFINITIONS

verse-by-verse

WRITE OUT VERSE-BY-VERSE

KEYWORDS/DEFINITIONS

verse-by-verse

THEOLOGICAL/DOCTRINAL TRUTHS I FOUND

WHAT DID I LEARN ABOUT GOD'S CHARACTER?

HOW WILL I LIVE IN LIGHT OF THIS TRUTH?

My Prayer Journal

| MY FAMILY | MY CHURCH | MY FRIENDS |

| MY COMMUNITY | MY NATION | THE WORLD |

pray continually

answered prayers

Read. Write. Love.
TRUTH

SPEAKER _____

DATE ____ / ____ / ____

KEY SCRIPTURES: _____ _____ _____

main points

WRITE OUT VERSE-BY-VERSE

KEYWORDS / DEFINITIONS

verse-by-verse

WRITE OUT VERSE-BY-VERSE   KEYWORDS / DEFINITIONS

verse-by-verse

THEOLOGICAL / DOCTRINAL TRUTHS I FOUND

WHAT DID I LEARN ABOUT GOD'S CHARACTER?

HOW WILL I LIVE IN LIGHT OF THIS TRUTH?

My Prayer Journal

_____ / _____ / _____

DATE

MY FAMILY	MY CHURCH	MY FRIENDS

MY COMMUNITY	MY NATION	THE WORLD

pray continually

answered prayers

Read. Write. Love.
TRUTH

KEY SCRIPTURES: _____ _____ _____

main points

WRITE OUT VERSE-BY-VERSE

KEYWORDS / DEFINITIONS

verse-by-verse

WRITE OUT VERSE-BY-VERSE   KEYWORDS/DEFINITIONS

verse-by-verse

THEOLOGICAL/DOCTRINAL TRUTHS I FOUND

WHAT DID I LEARN ABOUT GOD'S CHARACTER?

HOW WILL I LIVE IN LIGHT OF THIS TRUTH?

My Prayer Journal

_____ / ___ / ___
DATE

MY FAMILY

MY CHURCH

MY FRIENDS

MY COMMUNITY

MY NATION

THE WORLD

pray continually

answered prayers

Read. Write. Love.
TRUTH

SPEAKER _____

DATE _____ / _____ / _____

KEY SCRIPTURES: _____   _____

main points

WRITE OUT VERSE-BY-VERSE

KEYWORDS / DEFINITIONS

verse-by-verse

WRITE OUT VERSE-BY-VERSE   KEYWORDS / DEFINITIONS

verse-by-verse

THEOLOGICAL / DOCTRINAL TRUTHS I FOUND

_____
_____
_____
_____
_____

WHAT DID I LEARN ABOUT GOD'S CHARACTER?

_____
_____
_____
_____
_____

HOW WILL I LIVE IN LIGHT OF THIS TRUTH?

_____
_____
_____
_____
_____

My Prayer Journal

| MY FAMILY | MY CHURCH | MY FRIENDS |

| MY COMMUNITY | MY NATION | THE WORLD |

pray continually

answered prayers

Read. Write. Love.
TRUTH

KEY SCRIPTURES: _____ _____ _____

main points

WRITE OUT VERSE-BY-VERSE

KEYWORDS / DEFINITIONS

verse-by-verse

WRITE OUT VERSE-BY-VERSE

KEYWORDS / DEFINITIONS

verse-by-verse

THEOLOGICAL / DOCTRINAL TRUTHS I FOUND

WHAT DID I LEARN ABOUT GOD'S CHARACTER?

HOW WILL I LIVE IN LIGHT OF THIS TRUTH?

My Prayer Journal

_____ / _____ / _____

DATE

MY FAMILY	MY CHURCH	MY FRIENDS

MY COMMUNITY	MY NATION	THE WORLD

pray continually

answered prayers

Read. Write. Love.
TRUTH

SPEAKER _____   DATE _____ / _____ / _____

KEY SCRIPTURES: _____ _____ _____

main points

WRITE OUT VERSE-BY-VERSE

KEYWORDS/DEFINITIONS

verse-by-verse

WRITE OUT VERSE-BY-VERSE

KEYWORDS/DEFINITIONS

verse-by-verse

THEOLOGICAL/DOCTRINAL TRUTHS I FOUND

WHAT DID I LEARN ABOUT GOD'S CHARACTER?

HOW WILL I LIVE IN LIGHT OF THIS TRUTH?

My Prayer Journal

_____ / _____ / _____

DATE

MY FAMILY	MY CHURCH	MY FRIENDS

MY COMMUNITY	MY NATION	THE WORLD

pray continually

answered prayers

Read. Write. Love.
TRUTH

KEY SCRIPTURES: _____ _____ _____

main points

WRITE OUT VERSE-BY-VERSE

KEYWORDS / DEFINITIONS

verse-by-verse

WRITE OUT VERSE-BY-VERSE   KEYWORDS / DEFINITIONS

verse-by-verse

THEOLOGICAL / DOCTRINAL TRUTHS I FOUND

WHAT DID I LEARN ABOUT GOD'S CHARACTER?

HOW WILL I LIVE IN LIGHT OF THIS TRUTH?

My Prayer Journal

_____ / _____ / _____
DATE

MY FAMILY	MY CHURCH	MY FRIENDS

MY COMMUNITY	MY NATION	THE WORLD

pray continually

answered prayers

Read. Write. Love.
TRUTH

SPEAKER

/ /

DATE

KEY SCRIPTURES: _____ _____ _____

main points

WRITE OUT VERSE-BY-VERSE

KEYWORDS/DEFINITIONS

verse-by-verse

WRITE OUT VERSE-BY-VERSE   KEYWORDS / DEFINITIONS

verse-by-verse

THEOLOGICAL / DOCTRINAL TRUTHS I FOUND

WHAT DID I LEARN ABOUT GOD'S CHARACTER?

HOW WILL I LIVE IN LIGHT OF THIS TRUTH?

My Prayer Journal

MY FAMILY	MY CHURCH	MY FRIENDS

MY COMMUNITY	MY NATION	THE WORLD

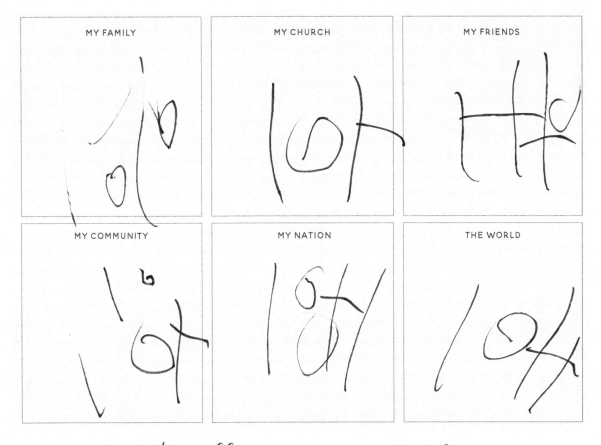

pray continually

answered prayers

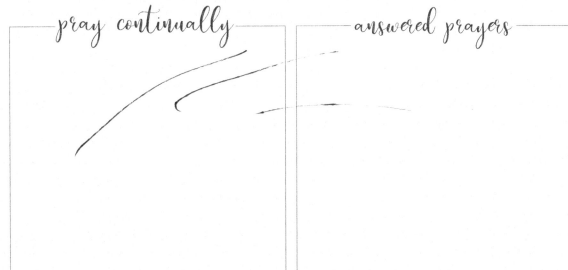

Read. Write. Love.
TRUTH

KEY SCRIPTURES: _____   _____   _____

main points

WRITE OUT VERSE-BY-VERSE

KEYWORDS / DEFINITIONS

verse-by-verse

WRITE OUT VERSE-BY-VERSE   KEYWORDS/DEFINITIONS

verse-by-verse

THEOLOGICAL/DOCTRINAL TRUTHS I FOUND

WHAT DID I LEARN ABOUT GOD'S CHARACTER?

HOW WILL I LIVE IN LIGHT OF THIS TRUTH?

My Prayer Journal

___/___/___
DATE

MY FAMILY

MY CHURCH

MY FRIENDS

MY COMMUNITY

MY NATION

THE WORLD

pray continually

answered prayers

Read. Write. Love.
TRUTH

SPEAKER _____

DATE _____ / _____ / _____

KEY SCRIPTURES: _____ _____ _____

main points

WRITE OUT VERSE-BY-VERSE

KEYWORDS / DEFINITIONS

verse-by-verse

WRITE OUT VERSE-BY-VERSE

KEYWORDS/DEFINITIONS

verse-by-verse

THEOLOGICAL/DOCTRINAL TRUTHS I FOUND

WHAT DID I LEARN ABOUT GOD'S CHARACTER?

HOW WILL I LIVE IN LIGHT OF THIS TRUTH?

My Prayer Journal

MY FAMILY	MY CHURCH	MY FRIENDS

MY COMMUNITY	MY NATION	THE WORLD

pray continually

answered prayers

Read. Write. Love.
TRUTH

SPEAKER _____   DATE ___ / ___ / ___

KEY SCRIPTURES: _____ _____ _____

main points

WRITE OUT VERSE-BY-VERSE

KEYWORDS / DEFINITIONS

verse-by-verse

WRITE OUT VERSE-BY-VERSE

KEYWORDS/DEFINITIONS

verse-by-verse

THEOLOGICAL/DOCTRINAL TRUTHS I FOUND

WHAT DID I LEARN ABOUT GOD'S CHARACTER?

HOW WILL I LIVE IN LIGHT OF THIS TRUTH?

My Prayer Journal

MY FAMILY	MY CHURCH	MY FRIENDS

MY COMMUNITY	MY NATION	THE WORLD

pray continually

answered prayers

Read. Write. Love.
TRUTH

SPEAKER _____

DATE _____ / _____ / _____

KEY SCRIPTURES: _____

main points

WRITE OUT VERSE-BY-VERSE

KEYWORDS / DEFINITIONS

verse-by-verse

WRITE OUT VERSE-BY-VERSE   KEYWORDS / DEFINITIONS

verse-by-verse

THEOLOGICAL / DOCTRINAL TRUTHS I FOUND

WHAT DID I LEARN ABOUT GOD'S CHARACTER?

HOW WILL I LIVE IN LIGHT OF THIS TRUTH?

My Prayer Journal

MY FAMILY	MY CHURCH	MY FRIENDS

MY COMMUNITY	MY NATION	THE WORLD

pray continually

answered prayers

Read. Write. Love.
TRUTH

SPEAKER _____

DATE ___ / ___ / ___

KEY SCRIPTURES: _____ _____ _____

main points

WRITE OUT VERSE-BY-VERSE

KEYWORDS/DEFINITIONS

verse-by-verse

WRITE OUT VERSE-BY-VERSE   KEYWORDS/DEFINITIONS

verse-by-verse

THEOLOGICAL/DOCTRINAL TRUTHS I FOUND

WHAT DID I LEARN ABOUT GOD'S CHARACTER?

HOW WILL I LIVE IN LIGHT OF THIS TRUTH?

My Prayer Journal

MY FAMILY

MY CHURCH

MY FRIENDS

MY COMMUNITY

MY NATION

THE WORLD

pray continually

answered prayers

Read. Write. Love.
TRUTH

SPEAKER _____ DATE ___ / ___ / ___

KEY SCRIPTURES: _____ _____

main points

WRITE OUT VERSE-BY-VERSE

KEYWORDS / DEFINITIONS

verse-by-verse

WRITE OUT VERSE-BY-VERSE

KEYWORDS/DEFINITIONS

verse-by-verse

THEOLOGICAL/DOCTRINAL TRUTHS I FOUND

WHAT DID I LEARN ABOUT GOD'S CHARACTER?

HOW WILL I LIVE IN LIGHT OF THIS TRUTH?

My Prayer Journal

_____ / _____ / _____

DATE

MY FAMILY	MY CHURCH	MY FRIENDS

MY COMMUNITY	MY NATION	THE WORLD

pray continually

answered prayers

Read. Write. Love.
TRUTH

SPEAKER _____   DATE _____ / _____ / _____

KEY SCRIPTURES: _____ _____ _____

main points

WRITE OUT VERSE-BY-VERSE

KEYWORDS / DEFINITIONS

verse-by-verse

WRITE OUT VERSE-BY-VERSE   KEYWORDS/DEFINITIONS

verse-by-verse

THEOLOGICAL/DOCTRINAL TRUTHS I FOUND

_____
_____
_____
_____
_____

WHAT DID I LEARN ABOUT GOD'S CHARACTER?

_____
_____
_____
_____
_____

HOW WILL I LIVE IN LIGHT OF THIS TRUTH?

_____
_____
_____
_____
_____
_____

My Prayer Journal

| MY FAMILY | MY CHURCH | MY FRIENDS |

| MY COMMUNITY | MY NATION | THE WORLD |

pray continually

answered prayers

Read. Write. Love.
TRUTH

KEY SCRIPTURES: _____

main points

WRITE OUT VERSE-BY-VERSE

KEYWORDS / DEFINITIONS

verse-by-verse

WRITE OUT VERSE-BY-VERSE   KEYWORDS / DEFINITIONS

verse-by-verse

THEOLOGICAL / DOCTRINAL TRUTHS I FOUND

WHAT DID I LEARN ABOUT GOD'S CHARACTER?

HOW WILL I LIVE IN LIGHT OF THIS TRUTH?

My Prayer Journal

DATE _____ / ___ / ___

MY FAMILY	**MY CHURCH**	**MY FRIENDS**
MY COMMUNITY	**MY NATION**	**THE WORLD**

pray continually

answered prayers

Read. Write. Love.
TRUTH

SPEAKER _____   DATE ____ / ____ / ____

KEY SCRIPTURES: _____   _____   _____

main points

WRITE OUT VERSE-BY-VERSE   KEYWORDS / DEFINITIONS

verse-by-verse

WRITE OUT VERSE-BY-VERSE   KEYWORDS/DEFINITIONS

verse-by-verse

THEOLOGICAL/DOCTRINAL TRUTHS I FOUND

WHAT DID I LEARN ABOUT GOD'S CHARACTER?

HOW WILL I LIVE IN LIGHT OF THIS TRUTH?

My Prayer Journal

MY FAMILY

MY CHURCH

MY FRIENDS

MY COMMUNITY

MY NATION

THE WORLD

pray continually

answered prayers

Read. Write. Love.
TRUTH

SPEAKER _____   DATE ___ / ___ / ___

KEY SCRIPTURES: _____

main points

WRITE OUT VERSE-BY-VERSE

KEYWORDS / DEFINITIONS

verse-by-verse

WRITE OUT VERSE-BY-VERSE

KEYWORDS/DEFINITIONS

verse-by-verse

THEOLOGICAL/DOCTRINAL TRUTHS I FOUND

WHAT DID I LEARN ABOUT GOD'S CHARACTER?

HOW WILL I LIVE IN LIGHT OF THIS TRUTH?

My Prayer Journal

MY FAMILY

MY CHURCH

MY FRIENDS

MY COMMUNITY

MY NATION

THE WORLD

pray continually

answered prayers

Read. Write. Love.
TRUTH

SPEAKER _____

DATE ___ / ___ / ___

KEY SCRIPTURES: _____ _____ _____

main points

WRITE OUT VERSE-BY-VERSE

KEYWORDS / DEFINITIONS

verse-by-verse

WRITE OUT VERSE-BY-VERSE

KEYWORDS/DEFINITIONS

verse-by-verse

THEOLOGICAL/DOCTRINAL TRUTHS I FOUND

WHAT DID I LEARN ABOUT GOD'S CHARACTER?

HOW WILL I LIVE IN LIGHT OF THIS TRUTH?

My Prayer Journal

MY FAMILY

MY CHURCH

MY FRIENDS

MY COMMUNITY

MY NATION

THE WORLD

pray continually

answered prayers

Read. Write. Love.
TRUTH

SPEAKER _____   DATE ____ / ____ / ____

KEY SCRIPTURES: _____   _____   _____

main points

WRITE OUT VERSE-BY-VERSE

KEYWORDS / DEFINITIONS

verse-by-verse

WRITE OUT VERSE-BY-VERSE   KEYWORDS / DEFINITIONS

verse-by-verse

THEOLOGICAL / DOCTRINAL TRUTHS I FOUND

WHAT DID I LEARN ABOUT GOD'S CHARACTER?

HOW WILL I LIVE IN LIGHT OF THIS TRUTH?

My Prayer Journal

DATE ___ / ___ / ___

MY FAMILY

MY CHURCH

MY FRIENDS

MY COMMUNITY

MY NATION

THE WORLD

pray continually

answered prayers

Read. Write. Love.
TRUTH

KEY SCRIPTURES: _____ _____ _____

main points

WRITE OUT VERSE-BY-VERSE

KEYWORDS / DEFINITIONS

verse-by-verse

WRITE OUT VERSE-BY-VERSE

KEYWORDS / DEFINITIONS

verse-by-verse

THEOLOGICAL / DOCTRINAL TRUTHS I FOUND

WHAT DID I LEARN ABOUT GOD'S CHARACTER?

HOW WILL I LIVE IN LIGHT OF THIS TRUTH?

My Prayer Journal

| MY FAMILY | MY CHURCH | MY FRIENDS |

| MY COMMUNITY | MY NATION | THE WORLD |

pray continually

answered prayers

Read. Write. Love.
TRUTH

SPEAKER _____

DATE ___ / ___ / ___

KEY SCRIPTURES: _____ _____ _____

main points

WRITE OUT VERSE-BY-VERSE

KEYWORDS / DEFINITIONS

verse-by-verse

WRITE OUT VERSE-BY-VERSE   KEYWORDS/DEFINITIONS

verse-by-verse

THEOLOGICAL/DOCTRINAL TRUTHS I FOUND

WHAT DID I LEARN ABOUT GOD'S CHARACTER?

HOW WILL I LIVE IN LIGHT OF THIS TRUTH?

My Prayer Journal

_____ / _____ / _____

DATE

MY FAMILY	MY CHURCH	MY FRIENDS

MY COMMUNITY	MY NATION	THE WORLD

pray continually

answered prayers

Read. Write. Love.
TRUTH

KEY SCRIPTURES: _____ _____ _____

main points

WRITE OUT VERSE-BY-VERSE

KEYWORDS / DEFINITIONS

verse-by-verse

WRITE OUT VERSE-BY-VERSE

KEYWORDS / DEFINITIONS

verse-by-verse

THEOLOGICAL / DOCTRINAL TRUTHS I FOUND

WHAT DID I LEARN ABOUT GOD'S CHARACTER?

HOW WILL I LIVE IN LIGHT OF THIS TRUTH?

My Prayer Journal

_____ / _____ / _____

DATE

MY FAMILY	MY CHURCH	MY FRIENDS

MY COMMUNITY	MY NATION	THE WORLD

pray continually

answered prayers

Read. Write. Love.
TRUTH

KEY SCRIPTURES: _____ _____ _____

main points

WRITE OUT VERSE-BY-VERSE

KEYWORDS / DEFINITIONS

verse-by-verse

WRITE OUT VERSE-BY-VERSE   KEYWORDS / DEFINITIONS

verse-by-verse

THEOLOGICAL / DOCTRINAL TRUTHS I FOUND

WHAT DID I LEARN ABOUT GOD'S CHARACTER?

HOW WILL I LIVE IN LIGHT OF THIS TRUTH?

My Prayer Journal

_____ / _____ / _____
DATE

MY FAMILY	MY CHURCH	MY FRIENDS

MY COMMUNITY	MY NATION	THE WORLD

pray continually

answered prayers

Read. Write. Love.
TRUTH

SPEAKER _____   DATE ___ / ___ / ___

KEY SCRIPTURES: _____ _____ _____

main points

WRITE OUT VERSE-BY-VERSE

KEYWORDS / DEFINITIONS

verse-by-verse

WRITE OUT VERSE-BY-VERSE   KEYWORDS / DEFINITIONS

verse-by-verse

THEOLOGICAL / DOCTRINAL TRUTHS I FOUND

WHAT DID I LEARN ABOUT GOD'S CHARACTER?

HOW WILL I LIVE IN LIGHT OF THIS TRUTH?

My Prayer Journal

MY FAMILY

MY CHURCH

MY FRIENDS

MY COMMUNITY

MY NATION

THE WORLD

pray continually

answered prayers

Read. Write. Love.
TRUTH

KEY SCRIPTURES: _____ _____ _____

main points

WRITE OUT VERSE-BY-VERSE

KEYWORDS / DEFINITIONS

verse-by-verse

WRITE OUT VERSE-BY-VERSE

KEYWORDS/DEFINITIONS

verse-by-verse

THEOLOGICAL/DOCTRINAL TRUTHS I FOUND

WHAT DID I LEARN ABOUT GOD'S CHARACTER?

HOW WILL I LIVE IN LIGHT OF THIS TRUTH?

My Prayer Journal

MY FAMILY	MY CHURCH	MY FRIENDS

MY COMMUNITY	MY NATION	THE WORLD

pray continually

answered prayers

Read. Write. Love.
TRUTH

SPEAKER _____   DATE ____ / ____ / ____

KEY SCRIPTURES: _____   _____   _____

main points

WRITE OUT VERSE-BY-VERSE

WRITE OUT VERSE-BY-VERSE	KEYWORDS / DEFINITIONS

verse-by-verse

WRITE OUT VERSE-BY-VERSE   KEYWORDS/DEFINITIONS

verse-by-verse

THEOLOGICAL/DOCTRINAL TRUTHS I FOUND

_____
_____
_____
_____
_____

WHAT DID I LEARN ABOUT GOD'S CHARACTER?

_____
_____
_____
_____
_____

HOW WILL I LIVE IN LIGHT OF THIS TRUTH?

_____
_____
_____
_____
_____

My Prayer Journal

DATE ___ / ___ / ___

| MY FAMILY | MY CHURCH | MY FRIENDS |

| MY COMMUNITY | MY NATION | THE WORLD |

pray continually

answered prayers

Read. Write. Love.
TRUTH

KEY SCRIPTURES: _____   _____   _____

main points

WRITE OUT VERSE-BY-VERSE

KEYWORDS / DEFINITIONS

verse-by-verse

WRITE OUT VERSE-BY-VERSE   KEYWORDS / DEFINITIONS

verse-by-verse

THEOLOGICAL / DOCTRINAL TRUTHS I FOUND

WHAT DID I LEARN ABOUT GOD'S CHARACTER?

HOW WILL I LIVE IN LIGHT OF THIS TRUTH?

My Prayer Journal

_____ / _____ / _____

DATE

MY FAMILY

MY CHURCH

MY FRIENDS

MY COMMUNITY

MY NATION

THE WORLD

pray continually

answered prayers

Read. Write. Love.
TRUTH

SPEAKER _____   DATE _____ / _____ / _____

KEY SCRIPTURES: _____ _____ _____

main points

WRITE OUT VERSE-BY-VERSE

KEYWORDS / DEFINITIONS

verse-by-verse

WRITE OUT VERSE-BY-VERSE

KEYWORDS/DEFINITIONS

verse-by-verse

THEOLOGICAL/DOCTRINAL TRUTHS I FOUND

WHAT DID I LEARN ABOUT GOD'S CHARACTER?

HOW WILL I LIVE IN LIGHT OF THIS TRUTH?

My Prayer Journal

_____ / _____ / _____

DATE

MY FAMILY	MY CHURCH	MY FRIENDS

MY COMMUNITY	MY NATION	THE WORLD

pray continually

answered prayers

Read. Write. Love.
TRUTH

KEY SCRIPTURES: _____ _____ _____

main points

WRITE OUT VERSE-BY-VERSE

KEYWORDS / DEFINITIONS

verse-by-verse

WRITE OUT VERSE-BY-VERSE   KEYWORDS / DEFINITIONS

verse-by-verse

THEOLOGICAL / DOCTRINAL TRUTHS I FOUND

WHAT DID I LEARN ABOUT GOD'S CHARACTER?

HOW WILL I LIVE IN LIGHT OF THIS TRUTH?

My Prayer Journal

_____ / _____ / _____

DATE

MY FAMILY	MY CHURCH	MY FRIENDS

MY COMMUNITY	MY NATION	THE WORLD

pray continually

answered prayers

Read. Write. Love.
TRUTH

KEY SCRIPTURES: _____ _____ _____

main points

WRITE OUT VERSE-BY-VERSE

KEYWORDS/DEFINITIONS

verse-by-verse

WRITE OUT VERSE-BY-VERSE

KEYWORDS/DEFINITIONS

verse-by-verse

THEOLOGICAL / DOCTRINAL TRUTHS I FOUND

WHAT DID I LEARN ABOUT GOD'S CHARACTER?

HOW WILL I LIVE IN LIGHT OF THIS TRUTH?

My Prayer Journal

MY FAMILY	MY CHURCH	MY FRIENDS

MY COMMUNITY	MY NATION	THE WORLD

pray continually

answered prayers

Read. Write. Love.
TRUTH

SPEAKER _____

DATE _____ / _____ / _____

KEY SCRIPTURES: _____ _____ _____

main points

WRITE OUT VERSE-BY-VERSE	KEYWORDS / DEFINITIONS

verse-by-verse

WRITE OUT VERSE-BY-VERSE

KEYWORDS / DEFINITIONS

verse-by-verse

THEOLOGICAL / DOCTRINAL TRUTHS I FOUND

WHAT DID I LEARN ABOUT GOD'S CHARACTER?

HOW WILL I LIVE IN LIGHT OF THIS TRUTH?

My Prayer Journal

_____ / _____ / _____

DATE

MY FAMILY

MY CHURCH

MY FRIENDS

MY COMMUNITY

MY NATION

THE WORLD

pray continually

answered prayers

Read. Write. Love.
TRUTH

SPEAKER _____   DATE ___ / ___ / ___

KEY SCRIPTURES: _____   _____   _____

main points

WRITE OUT VERSE-BY-VERSE

KEYWORDS/DEFINITIONS

verse-by-verse

WRITE OUT VERSE-BY-VERSE

KEYWORDS / DEFINITIONS

verse-by-verse

THEOLOGICAL / DOCTRINAL TRUTHS I FOUND

WHAT DID I LEARN ABOUT GOD'S CHARACTER?

HOW WILL I LIVE IN LIGHT OF THIS TRUTH?

My Prayer Journal

DATE ____ / ____ / ____

MY FAMILY

MY CHURCH

MY FRIENDS

MY COMMUNITY

MY NATION

THE WORLD

pray continually

answered prayers

Read. Write. Love.
TRUTH

SPEAKER _____ DATE _____ / _____ / _____

KEY SCRIPTURES: _____ _____ _____

main points

WRITE OUT VERSE-BY-VERSE

KEYWORDS / DEFINITIONS

verse-by-verse

WRITE OUT VERSE-BY-VERSE

KEYWORDS/DEFINITIONS

verse-by-verse

THEOLOGICAL/DOCTRINAL TRUTHS I FOUND

WHAT DID I LEARN ABOUT GOD'S CHARACTER?

HOW WILL I LIVE IN LIGHT OF THIS TRUTH?

My Prayer Journal

____ / ____ / ____

DATE

MY FAMILY	MY CHURCH	MY FRIENDS

MY COMMUNITY	MY NATION	THE WORLD

pray continually

answered prayers

Read. Write. Love.
TRUTH

SPEAKER _____

DATE _____ / _____ / _____

KEY SCRIPTURES: _____ _____ _____

main points

WRITE OUT VERSE-BY-VERSE

KEYWORDS / DEFINITIONS

verse-by-verse

WRITE OUT VERSE-BY-VERSE

KEYWORDS / DEFINITIONS

verse-by-verse

THEOLOGICAL / DOCTRINAL TRUTHS I FOUND

WHAT DID I LEARN ABOUT GOD'S CHARACTER?

HOW WILL I LIVE IN LIGHT OF THIS TRUTH?

My Prayer Journal

MY FAMILY	MY CHURCH	MY FRIENDS

MY COMMUNITY	MY NATION	THE WORLD

pray continually

answered prayers

Read. Write. Love.
TRUTH

SPEAKER _____   DATE _____ / ____ / ____

KEY SCRIPTURES: _____   _____   _____

main points

WRITE OUT VERSE-BY-VERSE

KEYWORDS / DEFINITIONS

verse-by-verse

WRITE OUT VERSE-BY-VERSE   KEYWORDS / DEFINITIONS

verse-by-verse

THEOLOGICAL / DOCTRINAL TRUTHS I FOUND

WHAT DID I LEARN ABOUT GOD'S CHARACTER?

HOW WILL I LIVE IN LIGHT OF THIS TRUTH?

My Prayer Journal

DATE ___ / ___ / ___

MY FAMILY

MY CHURCH

MY FRIENDS

MY COMMUNITY

MY NATION

THE WORLD

pray continually

answered prayers

Read. Write. Love.
TRUTH

SPEAKER _____   DATE ___ / ___ / ___

KEY SCRIPTURES: _____ _____

main points

WRITE OUT VERSE-BY-VERSE

KEYWORDS / DEFINITIONS

verse-by-verse

WRITE OUT VERSE-BY-VERSE

KEYWORDS / DEFINITIONS

verse-by-verse

THEOLOGICAL / DOCTRINAL TRUTHS I FOUND

WHAT DID I LEARN ABOUT GOD'S CHARACTER?

HOW WILL I LIVE IN LIGHT OF THIS TRUTH?

My Prayer Journal

DATE ____ / ____ / ____

MY FAMILY	MY CHURCH	MY FRIENDS

MY COMMUNITY	MY NATION	THE WORLD

pray continually

answered prayers

Read. Write. Love.
TRUTH

SPEAKER _____

DATE _____ / _____ / _____

KEY SCRIPTURES: _____ _____ _____

main points

WRITE OUT VERSE-BY-VERSE

KEYWORDS / DEFINITIONS

verse-by-verse

WRITE OUT VERSE-BY-VERSE   KEYWORDS/DEFINITIONS

verse-by-verse

THEOLOGICAL/DOCTRINAL TRUTHS I FOUND

WHAT DID I LEARN ABOUT GOD'S CHARACTER?

HOW WILL I LIVE IN LIGHT OF THIS TRUTH?

My Prayer Journal

_____ / _____ / _____

DATE

MY FAMILY	MY CHURCH	MY FRIENDS

MY COMMUNITY	MY NATION	THE WORLD

pray continually

answered prayers

Read. Write. Love.
TRUTH

/ /

KEY SCRIPTURES:

main points

WRITE OUT VERSE-BY-VERSE

KEYWORDS / DEFINITIONS

verse-by-verse

WRITE OUT VERSE-BY-VERSE

KEYWORDS/DEFINITIONS

verse-by-verse

THEOLOGICAL/DOCTRINAL TRUTHS I FOUND

WHAT DID I LEARN ABOUT GOD'S CHARACTER?

HOW WILL I LIVE IN LIGHT OF THIS TRUTH?

My Prayer Journal

MY FAMILY

MY CHURCH

MY FRIENDS

MY COMMUNITY

MY NATION

THE WORLD

pray continually

answered prayers

Read. Write. Love.
TRUTH

SPEAKER _____

DATE ___/___/___

KEY SCRIPTURES: _____ _____ _____

main points

WRITE OUT VERSE-BY-VERSE

KEYWORDS/ DEFINITIONS

verse-by-verse

WRITE OUT VERSE-BY-VERSE   KEYWORDS / DEFINITIONS

verse-by-verse

THEOLOGICAL / DOCTRINAL TRUTHS I FOUND

WHAT DID I LEARN ABOUT GOD'S CHARACTER?

HOW WILL I LIVE IN LIGHT OF THIS TRUTH?

My Prayer Journal

/ /

DATE

MY FAMILY	MY CHURCH	MY FRIENDS

MY COMMUNITY	MY NATION	THE WORLD

pray continually

answered prayers

Read. Write. Love.
TRUTH

SPEAKER _____   DATE _____ / _____ / _____

KEY SCRIPTURES: _____ _____ _____

main points

WRITE OUT VERSE-BY-VERSE

KEYWORDS / DEFINITIONS

verse-by-verse

WRITE OUT VERSE-BY-VERSE

KEYWORDS / DEFINITIONS

verse-by-verse

THEOLOGICAL / DOCTRINAL TRUTHS I FOUND

WHAT DID I LEARN ABOUT GOD'S CHARACTER?

HOW WILL I LIVE IN LIGHT OF THIS TRUTH?

My Prayer Journal

_____ / _____ / _____

DATE

MY FAMILY	MY CHURCH	MY FRIENDS

MY COMMUNITY	MY NATION	THE WORLD

pray continually

answered prayers

Read. Write. Love.
TRUTH

SPEAKER _____

DATE _____ / _____ / _____

KEY SCRIPTURES: _____

main points

WRITE OUT VERSE-BY-VERSE

KEYWORDS / DEFINITIONS

verse-by-verse

WRITE OUT VERSE-BY-VERSE

KEYWORDS / DEFINITIONS

verse-by-verse

THEOLOGICAL / DOCTRINAL TRUTHS I FOUND

WHAT DID I LEARN ABOUT GOD'S CHARACTER?

HOW WILL I LIVE IN LIGHT OF THIS TRUTH?

My Prayer Journal

MY FAMILY	MY CHURCH	MY FRIENDS

MY COMMUNITY	MY NATION	THE WORLD

pray continually

answered prayers

Made in the USA
Columbia, SC
10 September 2020

19815505R00083